Dancing Over Cheviot

Noel Hodgson

Noel Hodgson

The Reiver Press

The Reiver Press
The Old School House, Tillmouth,
Cornhill-on-Tweed,
Northumberland TD12 4UT

First published in Great Britain by The Reiver Press, 2008

www.noelhodgson.co.uk

A CIP catalogue record for this book is available from the British Library.

ISBN 0-9545181-1-X

Printed and bound in Great Britain
by Martins The Printers of Berwick-upon-Tweed.

This book is dedicated to
Judith, Robynne, Guy and Mother;
and to others of our family,
here and away.

I wish to acknowledge the following people
for their valuable help and support:

Kevin Temple, for the use of his photographs,
his company on our journeys,
and his passion for stories and people.

Bill Grisdale, graphic and creative designer
with a willingness and desire to produce a book
worthy of its place.

Dave White, whose belief and editorial skills
have encouraged a precision and trueness
in my writing.

I'm also indebted to the numerous friends and acquaintances
who have invoked and stimulated these poems.
Their affection, interest and company reflects
in my life's good fortune.

Standing
Among dead leaves,
My devotion to dreams
Is unspectacular.
I wear no armour
And carry no sword.

Alec Mallen, my Great Uncle, once shepherded at Cheswick. It's a wonderful, deserted spot that was much used – and guarded – during World War Two. Cromwell stayed here overnight on his march north into Scotland, in 1648. Beethoven, born in Bonn in 1770, would have been 235 years old on the day of our walk, 16 December 2005, which makes me a mere lad.

CHESWICK

Beethoven's birthday,
And mine. We wander down
On to the huge, deserted beach,
Bigger than the strip of sea half a mile away.

Not another soul in sight;
Only the glint of a distant car
Slipping across the causeway to Lindisfarne,
And northwards, Berwick, clinging to its slope.

Over sand, raked and swept
By tide and wind, we approach the water's edge,
Ruffled by small, harmless waves.

In a lowering sun,
The sky is stroked by a pink glaze,
Exerting a quiet, humming in our ears.

Save for the dead-seal hump of sacking,
This stretch of solitude, like his bare brow,
Wiped by the force of passion,
Is worthy of a joyful song;

'Happy birthday!'

Tommy Lumsden told me of this visit – and the radio's playing intrigued me. Noble Lands is the name of ground beneath Humbleton where, I believe, soldiers were buried (after the Battle of Humbleton, 1402). It's also the name he gave his house.

NOBLE LANDS

Tommy strolls along the dusky lane
Back to his childhood,
A derelict cottage beneath Humbleton.

Approaching, he hears music.
Curious, he steps inside,
Waking a tramp from sleep.

Tommy explains why he's there
And asks why the radio's playing.

"To keep the rats away,"
The other mutters.

"Not this one," Tommy grins,
Handing him a cigarette.

Soldiers, resting in retreat,
They blow smoke across the room,
No words needed;

Bold in each other's company
To dwell, alone.

Down Curly Lane we traipsed to school,
Onto the path above the road,
Knowing every good tree to climb
And, there, the fence rail we tightroped along.
Below stood Jimmy Fairbairn's farm
At the old mill, with doorsteps to leap,
Measuring our growth and prowess.

Next, spanning the River Aln,
The ancient two-arched bridge
Where we lingered daily,
Leaning over the shuffling water
Staring for trout in the shifting shadows;
Flood times tethered us longer,
Captivated by the tearing molten-brown
Overlapping the banks.

Lesbury Bridge

Crossing into the village we knew every house,
Best of all the sweet shop
Served by kind, elderly Mrs Mitchison;
I stole from her once and slept badly for a week.

Now, as I drive my family
Over the new, modern-designed bridge
With our Chinese takeaway from Amble's
Golden Harbour spicing the car's air,
I find it easy to be cynical
Of its loops of steel, like a fast-food logo,
Enabling motorists to fleet-foot across
A straighter, more vehicle-friendly route.

On our journeys back from school
I would often race home,
While my twin sister, Angela, would dawdle.
Later, I learned to appreciate her slowness,
My loitering with intent, under trees, at fences,
Old buildings — and bridges.

Retired, at last, the old stone bridge
With drooping eyes gazes upstream,
Towards the young pretender, its false wings
A symbol of the new century's ambition
To be noticed, different, admired.

And I wonder who, today, lingers over it,
Peering down into the shallows, feeling more
For what it gives than what it takes away?

The new bridge was opened in March, 2003. Its steel tubing is not structurally vital but is a design feature intended to catch the eye! Opinions differ as to whether it pleases or not.

Saturday, 17 November 1962, after returning from Rothbury Mart, shepherds Willie Middlemas and Jock Scott dropped off William Bullock at Castle Hill, then, against better judgement, attempted to reach home across the moor. At that time the road from Alnham to Ewartly Shank was merely a track and there was no telephone line. Their fate was revealed the following week. A police map of the accident marks where the tractor was abandoned and where the bodies of both men, as well as a glove and a sock, were found.

After this tragedy, the Northumberland Fell Rescue Team was formed, in 1963.

EWARTLY SHANK

Ewartly Shank

Like venturers
On a wild white sea,
The storm lashed them
With icy spray,
As desperately, across
The snow-blizzard moor
Their tractor lurched,
Until, swamped by drifts
It finally sank,
And groaned no more.

With abandoned curses
Both floundered homewards,
Stumbling, staggering,
Wearily entering
A deeper, burdening,
Vacant world.

A lost glove, sock,
The voice of a friend;
They perished apart,
Frozen in graves
Next week's sun
Gently opened,
To a gust of sorrow,
Rising and falling
Over the hills,
Like a gull's
Anxious mew.

In the whirlpool of Christmas Eve shopping in the city, the calm satisfaction that this man expressed contrasted plainly with the desperation the rest of us seemed overwhelmed by. There's a song entitled 'Christmas in Paradise' by the singer, Mary Gauthier, that I recommend heartily and which may have influenced my eye.

BIGG MARKET, NEWCASTLE

Bigg Market, Newcastle.

Around his scruffy shoes
Pigeons scuffle, like fish
Squabbling and jostling,
As he feeds them daily bread
From a paper bag.

Here, a man,
Face blotched and roughened
By a lack of self-care,
Offering his humble gift.

And while this shabby figure
Gladly feeds the birds
In his small, gracious world,
Christmas shoppers,
Caught in the current
Of seasonal goodwill,
Dart mutely by,
Desperately searching
For deliverance of joy.

Laura Veirs sang songs from her then-latest album, *Carbon Glacier*, which had been highly praised by pundits. In the small venue, her warm, amiable personality touched us all. After the show, walking back over the almost-400-year-old bridge with friends John and Graham Reavley, our mood was animated, stirred by the magic of the evening.

THE BARRELS ALE HOUSE

The Barrels Ale House

No more than thirty-five
Bunch inside the cellar bar,
Facing the small corner stage
Where bespectacled Laura Veirs,
From Seattle, gaily but modestly
Introduces her songs.

Intimately, her singing sails
Amongst us, like trails of mist,
Coiling words of innocence
And beauty, rejoicing in the seasons,
The sky, land, river and ocean;
Dreams and affection.

On the CD I buy, she writes,
'We love Berwick'.

Berwick by the sea.

As we wander out, late,
Into a lucid March night,
Crossing the old bridge
Above the shining water
Of the moon-silked Tweed,
A soft breeze refreshes
Our beer-cheery minds.

Gazing eastwards,
Beyond the flared estuary,
The star-flowered sea hums
A gentle chord, enticing feelings
Towards a mystical, rapturous world,
Where mermaids on every shore
Sing songs of tenderness
And glee.

George Wake was farm steward at Red Steads, Howick, when I worked there, briefly, after leaving school. As a young man he even ploughed with horses, and he once told me how, trudging up and down in boots, he would fold docken leaves between his toes to ease his burning feet. His skill and experience, working the land, was known and respected.

This poem resulted from my reworking of an earlier one – something that might have made George smile.

GEORGE WAKE

George Wake

See him now,
Woodbine in his mouth,
At the tractor wheel.
His stern face,
Silent, impassive,
Focused on the furrow.

Smoking in his cab
He trailed the ground,
Chorused by gulls
Feeding on worms.
Behind a bluntness
Breathed a warm, shy man,
Ambitious to please,
Neither fussy nor vain.

Fields were his trademark;
And along with the empty packets
He tossed out the window,
His days were measured
By labour and routine,
Returning, year after year,
To till and reap the land
Beneath his stewardship's
Keen, mindful eye.

In labour, wrapped in blankets,
They stretchered her off the moor
Down to the doctor's car.

Even now,
Over seventy years later,
She cannot forget the cold
Piercing her from below,
And a baby son who never
Came home.

Four more followed – three girls and a boy:
Effie, 1934; Heather, '38; Kathleen '44
(the only one born in the cottage)
And the youngest, Robert, 1947.

That severe winter of '47 still vivid:
"We were blocked in for ten weeks,"
Says Dulcie. "But we managed,
Though by the end the barrel, filled
With barley flour, was almost empty."

Four children and husband Matt;
Two pigs, two cows, two dogs,
Four cats – and hens, as well as sheep,
All to feed and care for.

Dulcie, small, brisk woman, constantly
Cooking and baking on the new range
(Moffat Bros Ltd, Gateshead),
While the fire, for the boiler in the kitchen,
Only stayed alight when the back door
Was left open, "No matter what time
of year," she adds, ruefully.

Memory shakes her head.

Maker of bread, butter, cream, cakes,
Scones and buns; produce
She sometimes loaded onto a bicycle,
To trundle off to local W.I. shows.

Brownridge

Once every month, groceries,
Ordered from Wooler store,
Finally delivered up from Chatton
On Jimmy Douglas's horse and cart.

"We often had people visiting.
Some stayed the night; somehow we made room."

Usually, Matt and she slept
In the bigger bedroom.
Only when a cow was calving in the byre
Would they switch to the smaller one,
So they might hear through the wall
Should they be needed in the night.

Every morning, Matt lugged up pails
Of fresh water from the spring well.
To feed his family, he dug another garden
For potatoes, beside the wood.

Matt, shepherd and master stick–dresser,
Spilling shavings onto the evening hearth.
(A shadow of a smile slips over her face.)

From 1932 to '54, 'Brownrigg' was home.
A simple, rigorous life, coping with work,
Yet rewarding years: children growing,
Thriving, learning. No one to bother them.
Basic but bountiful, a place to be proud of.

"I wouldn't want to see it now," admits Dulcie.
House a ruin, roof and walls crumbling.
She wrings her hands: "What a shame."

She'd rather remember it as it was.
Love keeping it standing.
Matt and she and four children,
Enjoying the fortune and freedom
Of their seclusion, with a heart humbled
By a child missing, cradled, silent,
In a far-off corner.

Dulcie
Anderson,
at ninety-
three,
described
their life
there.

I am indebted
to her for
sharing her
memories,
as I am to
Effie for the
line, 'Love
keeping it
standing'.

Sadly, Dulcie
died in 2006.

Regularly seeing these elderly ladies as I drive through Lowick, I began to make up a ditty-type song about them. In time, the lines developed and grew towards a more reflective piece, strung with time and its predictability.

LOWICK

Lowick

Two old ladies
Sitting on a bench
At the side of the road,
Watching folk and traffic
Passing by.

Mothers brushing
Doorways,
Turning to wave.

Couples strolling
Down the lane,
Arm-in-arm.

Youths mingling
At a corner,
Some smoking.

Children hop-scotching
On the pavement,
Summer-brown.

Two infants
In a seeded garden,
Staring up at wires
Beaded with swallows,
Soon gone.

The Kettley Stone, near Chatton, is unique to the area and not easy to locate, particularly in summer when the bracken is tall. The natural theatre in which it lies indicates its significance for tribal gathering and ritual. In addition to the nearby hanging stone, remains of the hill camp stand on the moor above.

KETTLEY STONE

Kettley Stone

Crouched,
Like a beast,
The rock squats
In the low hollow
Of the hillside;
Its humped back
Wreathed by a large,
Chiselled bowl:

An open womb,
Into which the drool
And sweat of a tribe's
Hunger for warmth
And survival,
Was cast and affirmed
In deathless stone.

Mighty,
Astride its shoulders,
Like aged chieftains,
Both sun and moon
Stir patient, potent
Shadows;

Returning dreams:

Whirl of dance,
Wild embrace,
Yells' delight;
Blood and breath,
Blazed and avid,
Quivering, like lightning,
In eyes, agape,
Sparked red.

A beautiful sunny afternoon in the market square, entertained by Folk Dance and music – the wonder of it enhanced by the performance of this figure's bounding joy.

Alnwick Music Festival

Music reeling, shimmers
In glaring sunshine,
Over an audience
That smiles and nods
Its appreciation.

On an open stage,
Dancers and musicians
Perform in costume;
Red, white, green and black,
Interweaving sound.

At the crowd's edge,
A tall, young man
Leaps up and down,
Lithe and rhythmic,
Like a Masai warrior
On an African plain.

Beside him,
His anxious mother,
Aware of heads turning,
Extends a hand.

He falters
Then jumps again.
In every spring
Rising with delight,
As if to rear
Above the numb walls
That cage his mind;
His beat of wings
A gasp of freedom,
Strange, elegant,
Moving.

Locally-based artist Olivia Gill involved children in an environmental art project about the Pin Well valley, near Wooler. It was ambitious and spirited, and the children who saw it through achieved an experience of learning way beyond the classroom.

The narrow valley was an ideal place for holding cattle markets and fairs, with its natural spring a focus for wish-making.

In earlier days, pins were a much cheaper option than coins for casting away.

PIN WELL

Pin Well

At the well
She sketches the children
Sketching the stones,
Wishing them well.

At the well
She imagines the children
Years from now,
Here like her,
With children.

And their children
Are staring into the water,
And they stare with them,
Attracted by the stardust
In the pool's lower eye;

And again, they reflect
Upon the truth and mystery
Of others who have stamped
This ground before them,
Pinning their thirst and dreams
Into the cupped, dripping hands,
Of this waylaid, ice-boned valley.

At the well,
She sketches the children
Sketching their wishes,
Wishing her well.

I was eating breakfast when I spied the bird; it was late September and the morning was as clear as glass. The sighting brightened my whole week. Learning about it was a real joy, until ...

Geoff Sample is a professional recorder of bird song.

GOSHAWK

Goshawk

Big bird on a branch
Of the tree
Commanding the garden.

Through binoculars
I stare, enthralled,
At its grandeur.

A peregrine?
I find a book. No.
It appears to be
A sparrowhawk,
Though larger.

Next day,
Geoff Sample says,
"It must have been
A goshawk."

Excitedly, I tell
More people
Than I can remember.

Then my brother, Danny,
Informs me they
Kill squirrels,
And the magnificence
Of it is blighted;
Like a girl
Who once charmed me,
Until I heard
Her spite.

Uncle Tommy

An early,
Solitary primrose
By the road,
I could have carried,
Had I known,
To where soon
You'll lie, beside
Your beloved.

Together,
You may again
Resume your pleasures
Of house and garden,
Walks on the shore,
Tennis parties
With afternoon tea,
And the kiss of Loire wine
Before evening meals,
Embracing in candlelight
Your life's devotion,
With flowers given,
Flowers received.

Unexpectedly, Uncle Tommy died late afternoon, Saturday
5 February, 2005. That day, walking with my mother, we spotted
a single, early primrose and I looked forward to telling him of it.

Jim

Tomorrow we'll bury Jim.
Mother will rightly weep again,
As she has done since he went,
Unwell, to hospital.

Crowds will gather at the church;
Farm folk, former rugby players, pigeon-fliers,
Friends from near and far.

Our family will shoulder a brave face.
His life will be recalled, as were others
Who left us before him.
We'll take courage in knowing
We celebrated and mourned them all
With our attendance, reflections,
Words of honour.

Jim, big brother, now so small,
Helpless, silent, will know nothing of it;
The regard and affection we hesitated
To declare while he was standing:

Simply because that's the way it is;
That's the way we are.

Beadnell church was crammed to the walls; another crowd was
gathered outside. Jim would have been embarrassed and moved
by the turnout, but glad at the way we filled up the Craster Arms
afterwards.

Bastard Heron had been involved in the murder of the Scottish Warden of the Middle Marches, Sir Robert Kerr, and to avoid arrest took flight as a wanted man. While I am no historian, I believe this event – John Heron's surrender; his local knowledge and advice – was pivotal, and served the idea of the flanking march which led, crucially, to an eventual English victory at the Battle of Flodden, 9 September, 1513.

Surrey House now stands dilapidated at the Haugh Head, outside Wooler.

SURREY HOUSE

Surrey House

Bordermen,
Who know them best,
Clear a road
Through the crowded camp.

On horseback,
At the head of his column,
Their weapons unloaded,
John Heron, sombre as a priest,
Leads his band towards
Surrey's banner, limp with drizzle
Outside the dwelling.

Offered his surrender
And service, the wise-headed Earl
Has guards escort the outlaw
Into the building, while he
And his two sons – the Howards,
Constable, Dacre and Stanley
Follow in attendance.

Once formalities are over,
They round a table
Where Bastard Heron's hand,
Like a spider, traces the map
With the cunning that has kept
Him free.

Ponderous and austere,
Old Surrey narrows his eyes
As a plan, carefully unleashed,
Glints in his mind,
Conceiving a victory no longer
Unlikely.

George Gibson and I have remained friends from early childhood. Our boyhood was stacked with play, sport and exercise, a legacy that has influenced our lives, even as we age.

We made this journey in the summer of 2002. It was a fine day and there was a familiar spring in our step as we looped the hill. The poem, read aloud, reflects the ebb and flow of our travel.

DANCING OVER CHEVIOT

Dancing Over Cheviot

Today, side by side, moving at pace,
Let's circle together over Cheviot's broad face;
Its slopes, hollows, mounds,
Our partners all the way.

From Mounthooly to Dunsdale,
We'll weave and glide upward, over and round,
A skip and a hop where rough heathers rise,
A leap and a bound where peat bogs lie.

Step for step, stride for stride, roving at will,
Pausing and turning to gather the view,
Shine and shadow brushing the ground,
Bedazzling our eyes.

Shoulder to shoulder,
Hearts beating in rhythm,
We'll float effortlessly on a sail of friendship;
Spirits singing, light as a breeze,
Enjoying the air, deliciously cool,
While we gambol keenly
Across the hill's wide, empty stage.

Though older and wearing,
A zest for adventure remains yet in our veins,
All from a love of childhood games;
The race, the chase, the climb, the ride,
Hide and seek, swing and slide:
So let's dance over Cheviot, springing with glee,
On legs, strong and sprightly,
Unfettered, this far, by the ties of age.

Cateran's cave – or 'Robber's cave' – on Heburn Moor is a natural underground passage to which steps have been laid, signifying its usability – as a possible shelter, hideaway, store or larder. Such cold places were adopted as ice rooms and this may explain the practicality of the steps. I've ventured down it alone, usually with a torch, and find it chilling but stimulating.

Perhaps Cateran was a local chieftain, like Ceatta from whom Chatton village derives its name.

CATERAN'S CAVE

Cateran's Cave

Down cellar steps I enter the hole,
Underground, and in deepening darkness
Edge forward, probing my way
Along the narrow passage,
Careful for my head.

A cold, damp air wafts over me,
Like a silent snarl, threatening my senses
With dungeon dread.

Further down I feel the squeeze
Of imprisonment and fears creep
Around me like invisible chains.

Here, in the black clutch
Of a moonless night, I sneak
Into the roots of my imagining,
Groping, like a robber,
For a glimmer of reward.

Back outside, above,
Enhanced by a bright, blue sky,
My eyes, wide open,
Prize the shining, freckled moor.

Berwick's town walls are architecturally splendid, built between 1558 and 1570 during Elizabeth I's reign. They also provide a wonderful retreat from the crowds. LS Lowry, the popular 20th century artist, often visited Berwick and painted many scenes, which are reproduced on the 'Lowry trail' around the town. I am pleased to learn that he enjoyed football as well.

BERWICK WALLS

Berwick Walls

I walk the walls around the town.
It's dull November and windy.
The sea appears ruffled, disturbed;
A grey, scowling face with a mean grumble.

Like Lowry, the Manchester artist
Who visited and loved the place,
I scan across the buildings, estuary,
Surrounding countryside,
Pencilling details in my mind
And consider the watchmen
During years of border strife,
On the lookout for invaders.

This afternoon Berwick Rangers,
By rights an English team,
Play at home against Cowdenbeath,
Whose Scottish fans are a zealous bunch,
As are the Saturday crowds below,
Thronging the high street for bargains.
Football and shopping: modern religions.

But up here on the walls, I'm glad
To be above all of that for a change.
My rushed, frantic self grabbing an hour
To withdraw from the scampering world;
Not detached, simply diverted,
Drawn to outline this modest picture.

Barter Books in Alnwick, one of the country's largest secondhand stores, is a huge success story from small beginnings. The building was once the town's railway station, where we boys arrived in the 'beetle' train from Alnmouth Station, going to see a Saturday matinée film at either the old Playhouse or the Corn Exchange.

BARTER BOOKS, ALNWICK

Barter Books, Alnwick

Humble in the shadow
Of Heaney and Hughes,
'Below Flodden' at £7.50,
Secondhand;

£1.55 more
Than buying new
In other shops.

Secretly,
It felt an honour
To line up with two greats;
A local player standing
Between two internationals.

Self-consciously,
I removed my book,
Placing it conspicuously
On another shelf.

Returning
A few weeks later,
I noticed with amusement
Both Heaney and Hughes,
Still there.

OPENING HOURS.
SUNDAY   7.30pm - 10pm
TUESDAY   7.30pm - 10pm
WEDNESDAY   7.30pm - 10pm
FRIDAY   7.30pm - 11pm
SATURDAY   7.30pm - 10.30pm

From the back cellar, Vera
Brings my beer to the passage counter,
Then follows me into the quiet room.

Only two regulars sit there,
On a bench against the far wall.
Pulling up chairs, we join them.

The room is basic, unadorned
By music, television, or games,
Offering only warmth, shelter, ale;
A chance to talk.

Such as
Who lives where, who married whom.
The threads of families unknotted;
What someone said, what was heard.
Events and histories dealt out
Like cards across the table,
Examined, considered.
The raw philosophy
Of how things stay the same
Before they differ,
But don't always change.

"He left round here t' start a new life,
But landed back inside a year."

"He always had a big opinion
Of himself, with little t' show for it."

"His old man was the same, always full
Of his own unimportance."

"Aye, he never met anyone
He liked better than himself."

The Star At Netherton

Momentarily, we nibble at the silence.

"I hear another car went through
The dyke again, at Burnfoot."

"Aye, it's a bad spot; I bet
Hardly any hedge there's not been tickled."

Gossip and beer, nudging each other,
Like old friends.

Vera, knitting in her grand chair,
Matroning our company
With a fervent eye,
Supervising her passengers,
As was the building's intent;
Designed for the railway
That never arrived.

A waiting room:
A pause between
Arrival and departure;
A refuge, safe in her proud hands,
Out of bounds to a loud-mouthed,
Senseless, mechanical world.

With our same jars refilled,
Each labelled by a coloured sticker,
We settle again into the haven
Of this sparse room,
Steeped in the luxury
Of thoughts and words,
Raised and drunk
Together.

For three generations the Mortons have owned The Star at Netherton. Its real ale is highly regarded, though many visitors are surprised to find the place is not quite what they expected. Choice is limited and food is not served. The toilets lie across the yard and a key is provided for their use.

In these commercial times, it is a uniquely individual place and Vera Morton is, without doubt, the star!

To create a poem about winter, I escorted the class outside, away from school, so they might observe firsthand and conjure images that they could carry back to their desks and develop in their writing. In order for them to avoid the constraints of rhyme, I discouraged it in their work, yet found myself struggling with the rhymes and rhythms used in my own poem.

POETRY LESSON

Poetry Lesson

We assemble beneath the wizened ash tree,
To consider ... whatever we can see, in silence.
Grey, knuckled, veined branches, twisted bare
By harsh winter wear, looking grave and glum.

Over the frosted road lies a cluttered farmyard;
Dead, rusty old implements, frozen hard and stiff.
In a nearby field, starlings sparkle in a huddle,
Swarming through icy stubble with hungry intent.

On Wooler cricket pitch, a leaden echo of games
Forgotten: Hogg, Tait, James, Clarke, Robson ...
Glistening above our small town, Humbleton Hill
Slumbers eerily still, its skull plastered with snow.

Reluctant to return to a stuffy classroom in school,
Norman Allan, playing the fool, skids onto his bum;
A wild clang of loose laughter at once chimes out,
And all about us in the air, invisibly, winter grins.

Across the Tweed in Scotland, Ladykirk church was built entirely of stone by King James IV, after he was rescued having attempted to ford the river. Some fifteen years later, on the march to Flodden, 1513, it took the Scottish artillery six days to bombard Norham Castle, under Anislow, into submission.

Among others, Elphinstone and Angus were reluctant to the invasion. A scorned Angus quit before the battle, though Elphinstone remained and was killed, unsaddled, like his king.

NORHAM CASTLE

King James alone dismounts,
Steps forward on the bank,
To stare across the louring water
Towards the castle's English flag.

He nods gently in recognition,
And signs himself with a cross,
In memory of his near-drowning,
Years ago, at this very spot.

Turning, he views his Lords,
Leaders of his great, invading army,
And fixes their attention into silence,
Raising both hands above his head.

"Content ourselves only when our banners
Are roused above those walls!" he implores.

A spirited cheer rises from the ranks,
Hailing his command.

Down line, astride his patient mare,
Elphinstone slowly shakes his head,
And mutters to himself,
"Beware the river's eyes, my King.
Last time you raised both arms here,
T'was death, unseated, you contended."

Catching the portent of these words,
Angus, craggy, at his side, spies the image
In the stream, and frowns upon
The omen's breath.

An ordinary, minor task, yet vital. I've always liked the saying, 'You never plough a field turning it over in your mind' – a useful prompt for action.

Joe Wealleans, who had worked on the railways, told me he'd had the can for over forty years, which also speaks of his care and attention.

MAIN STREET, NORTH SUNDERLAND

Main Street, North Sunderland

Wearing slippers,
Old fellow
Bowing at his gate
Tips up his can,
Oiling the hinges,
Catch and bolt.

Now, he swings
It open and shut,
Working in
The golden tears,
Freeing the stiffness
Of worn joints;
Shining the spur
That prods him
From his chair
On silver-buckled
Winter mornings.

I felt slightly guilty, not going to open the door for him and, concerned, watched him on his way. His brief performance was a delightful surprise.

NORTH ROAD, BERWICK

North Road, Berwick

In the queue
To pay for petrol,
I watch him turning
From the desk; an elderly,
Frail-looking man.

He meets my eye
As he shuffles slowly past,
Out the door,
Heading for his car;
A lady waiting
Behind the wheel.

Halfway there,
He comes to a stop,
And like an old, sick dog
Waggling its tail,
Wanting to please,
He raises his hands,
And weaving a little rhythm,
Hips slightly swaying,
He shimmies briefly for her
On the forecourt.

Through the windscreen
She smiles in amusement,
And from the shop window,
Radiating applause,
I display a wide grin.

In May, 2003 work began, dismantling his old cottage and building a larger house. Overseeing others and working conscientiously, Gerald Dickinson showed immense personal initiative and drive to accomplish his dreamed-of dwelling.

In addition to information about the Lancaster bomber, I learned about stone – and of the skills of those involved in the project, particularly the Turnbull brothers from Belford.

GERALD'S HOUSE

Gerald's House

Hearing his call,
I lower the stone onto the pallet
And hasten round to join him at the scaffolding.

'Look!' he points, eyes sparkling.

Low in the sky, like a giant dragonfly,
A Lancaster bomber is trawling
Towards us, its Merlin engines
Rumbling in our ears.

He tells me of the seven crew;
Cramped, vulnerable, daring,
Especially the rear gunner.

As the large, single aeroplane
Drones overhead into the distance,
We stand transfixed
By the example of ordinary men,
Their unthinking courage, grappling fate.

Afterwards, bending again to labour,
The remaining glory of this lone flying craft
Seems to fold itself around us,
Like dust in the air,
Quietly settling upon our minds,
For us to guard and share;
To stand proudly
Amid these walls.

To delay the execution of her father, Sir John Cochrane, imprisoned in Edinburgh for his involvement in rebellion against the early reign of James II and VII, Grizel, his daughter, in July 1685, robbed the postman of the signed death warrant. This delay allowed Sir John's family sufficient time to have him pardoned. The spot where, apparently, she waited in hiding is known as 'Grizzy's Clump', a cluster of trees south of Fenwick on the back road to Detchant.

There are differing versions of this exploit and its exact location.

GRIZZY'S CLUMP

Grizzy's Clump

Dauntless,
Hiding behind trees,
Grizel Cochrane
Disguised as a man,
Waits at dawn, pistol ready
Beneath her cloak,
For the clop of hooves
And panting breath.

Weary-eyed,
The mailman,
Trailing his mount
Toward the hill's top,
Ponders the wench
Who, early last evening,
Leaned at his side,
Raising his confidence
With whispers and ale,
Before, strangely, vanishing
From the room.

When, at once,
Leaping out like a ghost,
She snatches the reins,
Pointing her gun,
The rider, shaking,
Crumples to his knees,
Begging his life.
Then, stealing the letters,
She straddles his horse
To gallop away
Across Kyloe moor,
Streaked in mist.

Driving past with my sister, Angela, it came as a suprise and a delight to witness this occasion. We pulled up, for it was worth a photograph.

Local cricket is played by several village clubs in the district, though never at Seahouses. Bamburgh had a regular team for years, while Beadnell only lasted one season.

CRICKET IN SEAHOUSES

Cricket In Seahouses

While youths play cricket on the grass,
Passing motorists and pedestrians
Smile warmly at their fun.

Boys enjoying the sport of a game;
Informal, improvised, unregulated,
Simple, friendly play.

A whoop of delight at a swing of the bat,
Cheers for a catch, a wicket – applause;
Any derision erased by a grin.

Each player taking their turn
With good-hearted cheer,
Beneath an inert, flat sky.

In view, the Farne Islands,
Bamburgh and Lindisfarne castles
Easily dismissed by an unexpected
Common event:

Lads on a green,
Above a picturesque shoreline,
Rekindling a cool, listless day;
Reminding whoever cares to observe,
That true pleasure
Is best shared.

A Sunday afternoon, alone and listless, unable to stir myself from a pit of weariness. Strange that I should recall it and give it meaning.

CHATTONPARK HILL

Chattonpark Hill

A fine spray of snow
Scatters down off the branches,
As long-tailed tits flit
From tree to tree.

Up the hill, a dead tup;

Pulled out from below the fence,
Its bulging eyes reveal the terror
Of strangulation.

Sunday, weary Sunday.

Back to the TV.

No energy for work,
No vigour or feeling
For love.

The dead sheep, an accident,
Above the wood.

Three shepherds, Will Atkinson (right), Willie Taylor (centre) and Joe Hutton (left) were players of traditional Border music, greatly admired and respected by audiences far and wide. The three's honest good nature seemed to enhance their performances and folk artist Alistair Anderson, with others, ensured their lasting reputation by recording their playing.

WILL ATKINSON

Will Atkinson

As on a frosty winter's morning,
Resting by the valley stream,
He blows into the cave
Of his cupped hands,
His tune rising like linnets
From the tangled, yellow gorse
Into a sparkling May sky,
Sailing across green bracken
Where a scattering of Cheviot sheep,
Hearing strains of melody,
Lift their heads from grazing;
While at his side, panting in rhythm,
His two collies gaze up in adoration.

A lone shepherd, with his dogs
And mouth-organ,
Playing a merry, soulful song
To warm the toes of all
Who cherish the man and his music,
As natural as hill spring water,
Skipping and tripping along.

Friday, 9 September 1513, the English army, led by Surrey, left camp at dawn to flank round behind the invading Scottish army on Flodden hill. This manoeuvre forced the Scots to move toward Branxton where the battle was fought and where circumstances favoured an English victory. Losing their king, James IV, and many nobles among some 10,000 men slain, all Scotland was shocked by the terrible defeat.

HOWARD'S WAY

Howard's Way

This is the way they came,
The Admiral and his brother, the Earl,
From Twizel bridge over the Till.

This is the way their father followed,
Thomas Howard, Earl of Surrey,
Fording the river at Heaton Mill.

This is the ground the soldiers trudged,
From overnight camp at Barmoor;
Weary, hungry, sodden, sullen,
Faces pinched against wind, rain,
The cold cut of uncertainty.

This, my son, is the road they trooped
To fight the Scots, hearts quickening,
Nerves of each man thorned in silence,
Now and again, glancing for hope
In another's stare, on their grim path
Bound for fury.

And here we are today,
Some five hundred years later,
Born to this land,
Both well, without dread, tracing their steps
Southwards into a breezy, blue sky.
Unlike them, able to view and enjoy
The journey ahead;
Pallinsburn, Branxton hill, Flodden edge,
With the great tomb of Cheviot beyond,
Its snow-creased Bizzle gully,
Pale as a scar.

3 December 1863, a determined Eleanor Heron set off on her return journey from Alnham, crossing the moor – and home to Hartside, where her family awaited her. She failed to make it and some days later was found frozen, seated on a stone where she had stopped to rest. Her memorial at the spot declares simply that she 'departed'. I like the relevance of this understated word.

NELLIE HERON

Nellie Heron

Five
Children's faces gathered
Round the window,
Trickling tears of fear
And dread, like snow flakes
Melting down the outer
Breath-warmed pane.

Sitting here, mid-moor,
On a crystal-clear day,
Nellie Heron might have
Spied the far-off hilltops
Of Ros Castle or Simonside;
Even, perhaps, the glint of the sea.

Only, exhausted and shivering,
Head downcast in veils
Of driving snow, she saw
Nothing, save the vision
Of a lamp-lit sill,
With the departing waves
Of loved ones' strained
Good-byes.

A dull, cloudy January day, damp, windy and cold, making travel unpleasant. And then … a change in the light, and a scene that was both delightful and dramatic. I'd been to Wooler and had ordered a book by the late poet, Vernon Scannell, who'd also been a soldier and a boxer in his time. His influence somehow worked its way into this poem. Sam Baker is a Texan singer-songwriter whose bittersweet words resonate.

PAST AKELD

Past Akeld

Through thinning shrouds of mist
The low hills lie in amber light,
Like dipped sheep huddled cold
Between showers and rainbows.

On the glistening road, a lorry
Sprays muddy-red water
Over the car's windscreen.
Wipers wash off the gore,
Revealing a spectral figure;
A young woman on a bicycle,
Labouring along the highway,
Rain-slicked and burnished.

Looming above, an awning
Of giant cauliflower heads;
Brassy, cream-whipped clouds,
Smearing the vale in sepia tones,
Amplifying the wistful words
Of Sam Baker's melancholy song
Playing on the radio-cassette.

Like a boxer, slumped in his corner,
Gathering himself between rounds,
I lumber towards bouts of wonder,
Eager for the bell to strike;
To rise and fall, each time,
Overwhelmed by the blows
Of unassailable beauty.

The Battle of Homildon Hill, 2 September 1402, is referred to in Shakespeare's *King Henry IV, Part Two*. The Scots' leader, the Earl of Douglas, was wounded and, with many other nobles, taken prisoner. The Earl of Northumberland and his son, Harry Hotspur, with the Earl of March, were hailed victors but, within a year, Hotspur and Douglas joined forces against Henry at Shrewsbury, where they were defeated and Hotspur killed.

HUMBLETON

Humbleton

On top of his hill I surprise Jim Short,
Sheltering from a frantic wind,
His dogs rampaging around the cairn.

On a flat stone I squat down beside him.
We talk about weather,
Farming, local news.

We recall the day in September, 2002,
When a gathering of us celebrated
The battle's six hundredth anniversary;
How Jim in his jeep carefully rocked
The dowager Duchess up here
To the summit.

Shoulders hunched,
We view the slope below,
Where the assault took place,
Percy's archers spraying bloody havoc.
How 10,000 Scots, burdened with plunder,
Scrambled in turmoil as some 800 toppled,
Falling dead or wounded,
While others, harried and scoured
From here to the Tweed,
Were mercilessly slain.

By now, across this evening valley,
Buds of light open up,
Drawing down the growing darkness.

In the gloom, Jim and I descend,
Part company and head home.

Striding the road, I think of those men
Falling, falling more rapidly than the night itself,
Which had overcome us on the hill.
And as the vexed wind clips my ears
With sounds of frenzy,
I start to run.

Above Ford Moss, overlooking the Till valley and the Cheviots, the lone pine tree is a landmark in the lives of all those who dwell upon it. Standing on their own, such trees seem to possess a presence and spirit.

THE LONE TREE

The Lone Tree

We all can see
The lone tree;
It invites the eye,
Makes us stare,
Makes us wonder,
Heave a sigh.

Something about
The lone tree
Set against the sky;
Something to rely on,
There, until we die.

And if we stare,
It sees us too,
Inside and out,
Everything we do;
Day-time, night-time,
Eyes open, closed,
Always in view.

Something about
The lone tree,
On the ridge
Against the sky.
Something to rely on;
Lonely for us
Who dread life,
Blindly passing
By.

In 1667, the plague routed the village of Ancroft. The inhabitants, a thriving community of boot and clog makers, were devastated by disease. The trees are a memorial to the dead; they are a remarkable sight and a powerful reminder to us of the severe history embedded in our landscape.

ANCROFT

Ancroft

Sunlight streaming
Through a wiring of branches
Along a line of tall trees.

Already, the early rays of Spring
Chivvying rooks into loud nesting;
Another beginning, life promising.

There, in the buckled field
Between village and sycamores,
The plague's dying were carried out
To broom-bowered shelters,
Where each perished, alone,
Before the pyre was torched.

Today,
Almost a hundred trees remaining,
Standing, like war graves, a tribute
To the families of the fallen:

Boot makers for the military;

Footwear, cut with precision,
Created with craft and care,
Made to endure,
Expected to last.

The annual run of twenty miles first took place in 1957. For the fiftieth anniversary (a thousand miles covered) I was asked to write something, and imagining what I might say to Barbara Morris, a friend, to prepare her for the challenge, I wrote this poem. Barbara walked the course and despite blistered feet, reached the finish line. The fastest runner did it in just over three hours.

CHEVY CHASE

Chevy Chase

Take heed: no matter who,
No matter what, Cheviot shall sing
With open arms to greet you –
Hearts and lungs hauling heavy legs
On to its plain, bleak top.

Hedgehope, too, invites your strain,
Its rounded head nodding approval,
Cheering you on towards Langlee Crags,
Whose rugged salute will guide you
Down into the valley once more.

Here, both foes – fatigue and ache,
May hinder your climb along Carey Burn
Towards the final ascent – Hell's Path!
But beyond, Wooler Common beckons,
Urging you to a glorious finish.

And like Percy's flight from Douglas
Across these timeless hills, you also
May feel the reckless ground,
The thrill of pursuit and escape;
Gallant, breathless, burning joy.

Yet you, alone, should add
Your own stride to effort's ancient trod,
Leaving a trail, memorably yours
Along the wind-scrubbed way,
Rallied by the howl and cry
Of
"Chevy Chase!"

Josephine Butler, born near Milfield, crusaded against the injustice towards women castigated and imprisoned by the Contagious Diseases Act. Through her tireless work and courage, Parliament eventually conceded and the Act was repealed. Later, after other campaigns for women's rights and status, she returned to live in her native Northumberland where she died, in Wooler, and lies buried in Kirknewton churchyard.

JOSEPHINE BUTLER, (1828-1906)

Josephine Butler (1828-1906)

From their cells
They watched her passing:
Refined, composed, delicate;
An educated lady, exuding
Class and distinction.

Like others before her,
She wished to inspect
Their confinement and treatment,
Assess their condition and health,
Their level of degradation.

What made her different,
She was a woman, like them;
Yet with a voice of conviction
Equal to any man's,
And a serene, silent regard,
Which included them,
Like that of a mother,
Whose help they could trust.

For that reason,
No prisoner spat abuse
Or contempt, as she walked away,
Her presence leaving behind
An air of courage over despair;
Affection rather than pity;
Understanding above judgement;
Hope haloed by belief.

Lord Collingwood, aboard the 'Royal Sovereign', took command after Nelson's death in the victory at Trafalgar, 1805. On his Hethpool estate he ensured oaks were grown, following his life's belief that British naval ships were reliably built from homegrown trees. From an early age, he is said to have carried acorns in a pocket, planting them on his country walks to secure this vision.

Apparently, the oak, (*Quercus robur*) does not produce acorns until it has grown for some sixty years or more, and only after a century-and-a-half is its timber fit for use. Collingwood's hopes were clearly long-term.

COLLINGWOOD'S OAKS

Collingwood's Oaks

Each time he knelt to plant an acorn,
He dreamt a tree, full-grown;

Robust, resilient branches, armed against
A billowing, stormy Northumbrian sky.

Their stand traced his path, charting
His course through manhood;
Living monuments to a gentleman
Of nature, land and sea:

Woods anchored on hillsides, braving
Savage Cheviot winds; ships, sawn
And hewed from England's timber,
Splicing through fierce ocean waves.

Serving king and country, his life
Was dutifully sown, pursuing
A belief in his nation's sovereignty;
Resolute, venerable, abiding;
Mighty as the boughs
Of the solid, trusty oak.

A line of electricity poles runs up the centre of the field like a spine. A strip of woodland on either side narrows its span before it widens out on to higher ground. As a vantage point there's generally little to commend it, but the fine new gate bestows value to it, and makes me pause in wonder. This morning I learned, counting by hand, that there are about sixty grains to every head of wheat. Also, the new gate of galvanised steel, supplied by Glendale Engineering, was made in the Telford area, West Midlands.

NEW GATE

New Gate

Up the road,
A new double gate, six metres wide,
Gleaming aluminium-silver, unblemished
By weather, creature or machine.

Seven bars high, it hangs perfectly
To rest my elbow and chin, as I stand
Peering across early, jade-coloured wheat,
Sniffing like a terrier dog for the scents
Of undercover life beneath the ripples
Of an evening breeze sliding down
From Harper Ridge.

Here, another window ledge
To spy on the invisible,
The unknown that lies out of sight;
To hunt, with the curiosity
Of an excited hound,
Across my thoughts' terrain
For growth and change;
Fresh, tangible learning.

The John Bull in Howick Street, Alnwick, remains a true local pub. Its selection of real ale, beer and whisky is remarkable. Gus is a character and entertaining, as well as professional in his role as landlord.

THE JOHN BULL

The John Bull

Gus gives us
A low look
As we arrive late,
Frowns at the clock
In a show of rebuke.

"Good morning, gentlemen,"
He says, pointedly.
"Now," he pauses,
"What's it to be?"

In a perfunctory voice,
He reads out the ales
Chalked on the board.
George sticks to lager;
For Fred, Peter and me,
It's 'Landlord's Choice'.

At seats round a table,
Beneath Gus's gaze,
We taste our beer
And discuss the smoking ban
That's come into force
Since we met here
Last week.

"Gus," gleams Peter,
Who likes to stir,
"Since the room's air
Is now cleaner,
And you must
Be smoking less,
I guess, already,
You're feeling fitter."

With a bitter brow,
Gus raises his chin.
"Indeed not, sir.
All this walking,
From the warm within
To the cold outside
Will be the death of me."

"Then give it up, man!"
Peter beseeches.
"Save yourself."

In a deliberate act,
Gus reaches behind
For his packet on the shelf.
"Normally, latecomers
Remain quiet and discreet."
He smirks, impishly,
"When I return,
I'll serve the other three."

At the table,
We allow a chuckle.
"Peter," I grin.
"When he comes back,
I dare you to joke
That it's him, not you,
That's been in-de-street."

A groan wafts
Across the room,
Thick as smoke,
And Peter's eyes
Light up.

I wrote this in 1992, long before the present hunt laws were passed. Who knows, the way things are heading, this notion may become 'reality'?

WINTER HUNT

Winter Hunt

Elsdonburn Shank

The hounds come running
Over the hill, bounding
Across the moor of snow.

Strung out in pursuit,
Huntsmen on quad-bikes,
Their engines snarling,
Clatter past.

No horses today;
Snow too hard and deep.

An odd, disturbing sight,
On a peaceful, sun-crisp,
Winter's forenoon.

Perhaps, some future day,
The fox, too, will be mechanised,
Panting to the throttle
Of a studio operator.

I took Guy and his friend, Jake, to see the waterfall in spate from recent downpours. The rainbow's appearance was amazing; their absorption absorbed me. In a world so contrived, for the young, this reality – a true experience – was most satisfying. Leaving the waterfall, we carved the boys' names on a tree, and then visited the nearby rock with its cup and ring marks. While I cut hazel sticks, they sat like natives, paring spears.

As the old adage has it, one swallow doesn't make a summer, but we'd seen a kingfisher on the Glen only weeks earlier and *it* did.

ROUGHTING LINN

Roughting Linn

Waterfall, swollen brown,
Plunges, crashing down,
Roaring white into the pool's
Dark chamber.

Poised on rock, both boys
Stare, eyes snared
By the torrent's noise
And cloud of spray, steaming
The air.

As if on show, sudden sunburst
Floods the shelter, slicing
A faint, slender rainbow
Through the misty vapour.

Mesmerised by its ethereal
Gleam, they gaze enrapt.

Without a TV or computer
Screen to distract
Or deflect their vision,
Nature's magic sword
Carves itself
Deep inside their wonder,
Just as a kingfisher's
Radiant sweep,
Made a summer
Splendid.

If seen on TV, Luke's feat would've made the world gasp. We were lucky.

LUKE'S GREAT SAVE

Luke's Great Save

It was noontime, November, a mild sunny day,
Glen House was playing Till, seven-a-side soccer,
Ten minutes each way.

The score was level, a keenly fought game,
When Glen's young keeper rushed out of his area,
Luke Strangeways his name.

Attempting a clearance he fell flat on his seat,
Miscuing the ball to Till's Warren Lumsden,
Skilled with both feet.

In the blink of an eye he showed neat control,
Aimed his shot truly, and gazed as it glided
Towards a clear goal.

But then into the picture, as swift as a hare,
Came Luke racing back, to hurl himself bravely
Up into the air.

Stretched out like Superman, he tipped the ball wide,
And everyone halted, mouths open in wonder,
The great shot denied

Applause followed loudly, faces beaming with joy,
Veins swelled, blood tingled, as Luke rose up grinning,
Our hero, a boy!

For those who were witness, age can never erase,
The magnificent sight of Luke's leap into space,
Performing his incredible, remarkable,
Miraculous SAVE!

A lovely stretch of beach between Seahouses and Bamburgh,
where we often go. Free to roam and play, we seemed to enjoy
the opportunity all the more.

BEACH AT GREENHILL

Beach At Greenhill

At Greenhill, we run down to the beach to play
Football on sand, smooth as a gym floor.

Inland, fields lie smothered in snow,
But here on the coast it's sunny and clear.

Reaching rocks we leave the ball
And wander out to the water line.
Head down, my son is fascinated
By weed-braided pools and limpet shells.
I kick one off to reveal its juicy inside.
Nearing the edge, turnstones stab at boulders
Dreadlocked by bladderwrack.

For a few moments, we smile again
At the illusion of an aeroplane
Taking off from Inner Farne.

On the retreat, he shouts for me to stop,
Bringing two small starfish in each hand.
We turn them over to observe their shiny,
Glistening underneaths, intricately designed.

Evening, at home; we read about limpets,
Turnstones, starfish, and learn that
Nothing should be taken for granted.
Each existence has a span of life
Dependent upon relationship,
And we ourselves are no different.

Father, son, together on a snowless beach,
Best of friends, for a day; one at a time.

Having known this friend since school days, it was a blow not to recognise him straight away. It was, however, pleasing to find his candour and cheerfulness undimmed, despite his condition. In this poem, I simply wanted to proclaim his strength of character and my admiration for him.

ALNWICK MARKET PLACE

Alnwick Market Place

Slipped through the arch into the mellow sunlight
Of the open market place.

Glancing at the tables outside the café,
One fellow sitting alone, tanned, gaunt,
Head shaven, smiled and stared.

I looked away, looked back.

He stood up in greeting;
The glint of eyes and grin welcoming.

Memory's door sprang open.
I called his name.

Seated together we drank coffee.
His long illness and treatment had stripped him down,
Like a moorland tree, mauled and shaken
By harsh storms, year after year.

Buoyed by our enduring friendship, we chatted and chuckled,
Catching up on news of family and friends.

Later, as he left, I watched him walk away.

Though slower and stiffer, I glimpsed the stride and swing
Of the lean youth and man I remembered;
The dashing, laughing cavalier with nerve
And a ready handshake.

At once, I wanted to shout out a stronger, final farewell;
Words which would ring out across the square,
Insisting, like a town crier, that everyone should know him.

Yet I didn't.

Before the battle, King James IV of Scotland resided at the castle. Lady Heron, whose husband William was held hostage in Scotland – in place of his half-brother, John Heron – would naturally be a welcoming hostess. Her dalliance with him is a matter of speculation, though in the end Ford Castle received no favours from him and was set aflame.

BEYOND FLODDEN

Beyond Flodden

The moon,
Like a half-closed eye,
Hangs low over
The shadow-robed hill.

The dark lid of cloud
Seems motionless,
But in minutes slowly lifts
And the full moon sneaks off
Beyond Flodden.

Over the valley a lantern
Shines outside Ford Castle.
A figure mounts his saddled horse,
Commanding others
Before riding away.

At her window, Lady Heron,
Sashed by dawn's mauve breath,
Gazes across the River Till
Towards the slope
Where Scottish campfires
Are being spiked alive.

Before noon,
When the building will burn,
She too will have left
With her possessions,
Laden by a bleeding,
Sunken heart.

A rare, relaxed occasion that hot summer when pressed by too
much that was mainly self-driven. TS Eliot wrote, in his poem
Ash-Wednesday, 'Teach us to care and not to care / Teach us to
sit still'. I was ready to do just that.

A HAPPY MAN

A Happy Man

I'm happy:
The boys are playing
On round straw bales;
A run and a jump,
Scrambling on top
To idly chat, munching crisps,
Before sliding down
To play again
In gilded sunshine.

I'm glad
It's made easy for me;
Bicycles ditched at the gate,
Alongside heartache,
Leaving me to lounge,
Blissfully, in this glazed
Summer field, arrayed
By sallow, arid hills,
Scribbling words
That are a blessing,
Right now, to no other
Than me.

At Bamburgh's War Memorial, my elderly mother remembered this story. Naturally, I was alarmed by the man's bravery and manner of his death, which, without her, I might never have known. I pondered the list of casualties, all, like him, relegated to a name from the past ... another time, another century.

Ernest's father, agent for Lord Armstrong, was architect of Armstrong House, which is now known as Abbeyfield. There the story was confirmed by Miss B Calderwood, to whom I'm grateful.

Ernest Bernard Lomas Hart, known affectionately by some as 'Boysie', died on 24 May 1940.

'BOYSIE' HART

'Boysie' Hart

Prisoners,
On a burnt, broken road
Near Dunkirk.

Captain Hart, appalled by guards
Striking one of his men,
Rushed to his aid.

For his trouble, unafraid,
They heaved him up
Against a wall,
Raised their rifles
And shot him dead;

A lesson for all.

Below Bamburgh Castle,
Inscribed in metal set into stone,
His name listed:
'Ernest BL Hart'.

No more said.

One of fifteen, all the same;
Trained to fight, taught to kill;
Soldiers passed on, out of sight;
Soon unheard, almost unknown;
Now, nearly forgotten.

'Boysie' Hart.
Died through kindness.
A hero, still.

A Wooler neighbour, unwell, had a short time to live. What can you say? Feelings of hopelessness were addressed by writing this.

The big tree, loved by birds, stands at the corner of our gardens.

'Keep a ha'd' is a Northumbrian valediction. I use it aptly.

SNOW

Snow

Fiercely,
The snow blows.
We go outside
To play in the garden.
The cold straps our bodies.
We cower and kneel
In the snow.

In a bare tree,
Black-cloaked crows
Glare down upon us.
Their soulless eyes glinting,
Growing colder.

Sinking deeper,
Our fears tremble.
But we are fearless,
Without woe,
For we have loved
Our lives, and loved.

With courage,
We haul ourselves up,
Climbing into the air,
Onto branches
Where, keeping hold,
We watch the birds
As they fall and perish
In the snow,
Too weak, too hopeless,
To raise their wings.

Bill Grisdale and I were deep in conversation and thought my son was still with us. According to Bill, my voice reflected my growing alarm, fearing Guy had drowned. It was a truly nightmarish experience, which even now makes me shudder.

LILBURN POND

Lilburn Pond

Talking, we walked round
The bend of the large pond
Into the trees, never thinking
He wasn't with us until we
Stopped at the other side.

Turning, I called for him,
Then called for him again.
Anxious, I shouted,
Then shouted again.
Fearful, I hurried back,
Breaking into a run,
Bellowing.

Where he'd last been with us
I screamed out his name,
Over and over again,
And scanning the surface,
My chest rioted in panic.

Suddenly, across the water
I spotted his blond head
Bobbing among shallow reeds;
Hunting for toads and frogs.

Overcome with relief, I sank
To the ground and lay motionless;
Staring heavenward,
Tears clouded my eyes.

The controversial issue of local wind farms continues; the debate centres upon their environmental value weighed against their blighting of the landscape – in the manner of the electricity pylons that stalk through the county.

WHITE INVADERS

White Invaders

Peering northwards
From my English window,
A band of brazen sunlight
Strikes up the Scottish hills.

Alarmingly,
Some twenty miles away,
A cluster of wind turbines
Disclose themselves,
Like border invaders,
Brandishing twirling blades.

Immediately, I reach
For the phone.

Within twelve months (2003-2004) these three events occurred, with the element of good fortune linking them together.

LUCKY WOOLER

Lucky Wooler

A sunny, mellow October day;
The Wheatsheaf Hotel, smouldering.
Drinkers in the bar, lapping their beer,
While upstairs, unknown to them,
An electric heater sparks into flame,
Gnawing rapidly through room and roof;
The alarm is raised by folk outside,
And all emerge, not a single hair singed.

And Mr Ancrum, at eighty-nine,
His foot jammed on the accelerator,
Careering out from Mike Hope's forecourt
Onto the A697, and back, leaving a trail
Of destruction, halting, with a crunch,
In Bob the Builder's solid, stone porch;
Neither Mr Ancrum, his two passengers,
Nor any other, breaking a single bone.

Then, Barclays Bank cash machine
Doubling your money; everyone a winner!
Opportunists pouncing, like jackals
For the kill, posting the town's name
Throughout the kingdom, and beyond.
Celebrants and purists alike, amazed
By the bank's limp, compliant stance;
No one forced to return a single penny.

A bright, magical, starry midnight, the hills round Kilham aglow.
The dead fox, at rest on the tarmac.

ASLEEP

Asleep

Beneath
A full moon,
A fox, on its side,
Lying dead
On the road,
As if sleeping,
Peacefully.

It's late,
I'm driving home.

Soon,
In bed, asleep,
Dreaming;

The fox rising,
Stretching,
Limping away
Across the valley;
An orange
Copper flame,
Shimmering
Between coals
In the night's fire.

The quiet road between Elford and Burton is one of many we travel on our gentle strolls. Acutely aware of the loss of my brother and uncle that same year, their presence was imagined. At ninety-one, mother, on good days, belied her age, stepping out.

BACK ROAD

Back Road

Two shadows
Ghost the grey hedge
Before us.

Mother and I
On a lonely, back road,
Pausing to admire
A skein of geese,
Noisy as children,
Ripple across
A pale, silk sky.

Then, at a gate
Tilted seaward;
Gazing over bare,
Brown fields
Slashed and scraped
By the sun's sharp blade.

Led by shadows,
Mother and I
Slowly pass a winter's
Ember afternoon;
Now and again,
The four of us,
Raising our heads
To pave our way's
Farewell.

AWAY

WITH MY FIRST BOOK, *Below Flodden*, the combination of poetry, prose and photographs seems to have proven popular with many readers, from near and far. This new collection, freshly clothed, continues in similar vein.

While *Dancing Over Cheviot* repeats its predecessor's depiction of characters, places and events drawn from my life here in north Northumberland, it was necessary in this second book to give it an appearance all of its own. After all, the poems are new – or more recent reworkings of older writing that has lain in notebooks, unfinished, until now; the poem about George Wake, smoking on his tractor, was first drafted as early as February 1974.

Once more, design and circumstance have turned my attention toward scenes and subjects that might easily have been passed by or ignored.

The 'Boysie Hart' story was a revelation that I felt compelled to record, whereas 'Alnwick Music Festival', 'Humbleton Hill', 'Bigg Market, Newcastle' and others were drawn from accidental encounters worth developing through my desire to hold on to them.

Other poems such as 'Ancroft', 'Collingwood's Oaks' and 'Josephine Butler' arose from my interest in local history. Flodden's battle and its story continues to evoke powerful images in me. John Heron, the outlaw, handing himself over to the Earl of Surrey at the English camp near Wooler was a significant moment, and I imagined how the wily old Surrey saw him as a vital ally in the contest against the larger Scottish army. The siege at Norham and Lady Heron's predicament at Ford Castle were other dramas that I wished to include.

Of course, some poems proved easier to accomplish than others, but it always comes as a relief and a joy when each is completed to my own satisfaction. It's perhaps no surprise to say that my favourite, or should I say the poem I'm closest to, is always the one I'm busy working on.

At the end of a talk I gave to a Local History group in North Sunderland, I was asked what had prompted me to write in the first place. "An inability," I replied, for it was always difficult for me as a young man, in any discussion, to express myself adequately. Whereas, on the page, there was time to consider and shape the sentences I wished to speak; the arrangement of words, to create images and meanings, became a fascination. And since then, reading and hearing writers, poets and singers whose words flare before me is a cause for joy.

For anyone travelling through this most northernly corner of England, there are many features of the past clearly visible to those who care to pause, admire and learn. There are, however, a number, such as Nellie Heron's stone, Cateran's cave and the Kettley stone, that are less conspicuous and require a greater effort to find them.

Having been born and raised in north Northumberland, my connection with its places and people is intimate, as my poem 'Lesbury Bridge' exemplifies. And without the company and friendship of Dulcie Anderson, Vera Morton and Tommy Lumsden, for example, the poems 'Brownridge', 'The Star At Netherton' and 'Noble Lands' could not have been written as they now stand.

It was during a lesson at Glendale School, when I referred to the Ewartly Shank tragedy, that a pupil, Craig Scott, informed me he was grandson to Jock Scott, one of the lost shepherds. Kindly, Craig brought me detailed information about the incident, resulting later in the poem.

Although I didn't know the young man whom I'd seen jumping up and down at Alnwick Music Festival, when Kevin Temple read my poem he guessed who it was and asked if he could show the piece to the lad's mother. I was happy for him to do so and was later delighted to hear the poem that the lad's father had himself written, about his son as a child.

As in *Below Flodden* I have included poems about people whom I have known and admired – people like George Wake and Will Atkinson. Two or three months before my friend Derek Alder died, he read my poem about our chance meeting in Alnwick's market place. Unlike my brother, Jim, Derek was able to reflect upon the tribute that I'd felt was his due.

The current issue concerning the building of wind farms in the area sprang up in the 'White Invaders' poem. Whether or not the wind turbines are viable here is debatable, but it's important to remember that what makes this area attractive to visitors – and to we inhabitants – is its relatively unspoilt beauty. There are blemishes already that act as a warning to further disfigurement.

No matter how I view it, the new bridge at Lesbury seems out of place and, however necessary (so we're told) is the rapid development of housing and amenities such as caravan parks, it does make me fear for what the future holds. My reservations were roughly reconciled in a poem I scribbled down while sitting on Yearle hill a few years ago, overlooking the Heugh Head valley. Faced with the hum of evening traffic on the A697, the high fence of pylon cables and the extending tongue of the caravan park below, I found myself hurriedly turning away to the hills for peace of mind.

Throughout my years, I have been privileged to enjoy the loveliness and freedom of this area. I certainly don't wish to turn my back on it – to look elsewhere for inspiration; I am rooted to it, grown and fruited, and I'm disturbed by changes that erode the charm and spirit of our communities and landscape. Too often, I hear the shout for progress as a decoy for gain. We have a duty to preserve its splendour.

The title poem, 'Dancing Over Cheviot', is testimony to a special day out with a life-long friend, George Gibson. Two weeks after our trip over Cheviot hill I saw him dancing at a party, at Alnwick Rugby Club, and the title for the poem was struck. Like the adventure of that day, compiling this second collection of poetry has been a hike of pleasure, and consequently, it seemed an ideal name for the book, in which I have aimed to vary the rhythm, pace and tone of my writing, as in the steps of that journey. Incidently, both individual poems, 'Dancing Over Cheviot' and 'Chevy Chase' benefit, I believe, when read aloud and the force and flow of the lines are stressed.

Many years ago, I went to Newcastle to see Sonny Liston, at the time heavyweight boxing champion of the world, giving a training exhibition in St James's Hall. As well as sparring, he demonstrated a precise, skipping routine to music, which I watched in awe and which has proven a catalyst throughout my career, teaching PE and Drama – movement and rhythm being powerful stimuli.

Although rhyming poetry is popular, I don't find myself fully drawn to it, despite the good natured criticism of friends who are. For one, it's not as simple as it looks and, secondly, a rigid structuring of lines tends to inhibit the scope of my writing that free verse allows. I suppose, in a way, it's the 'song' of the words strung together which attracts me – the rhythms more than the rhyme. Having said that, 'Luke's Great Save' and 'Poetry Lesson' are a combination of the two and, bound by their own rules, they both proved difficult to complete. Hopefully, I've eventually done them justice.

Local news is, of course, the domain of our newspapers, the *Berwick Advertiser* and *Northumberland Gazette*. In a different way, I suppose, focusing my writing on this small part of the county, as I do, often subjectively, is another form of reporting, too. In 'Lucky Wooler', the three incidents were at their time very much in the news, and by connecting them through fortune, I hoped to chronicle them in an interesting way.

Despite a close interest in dialect and accent, I prefer, in writing my poems, to avoid using the vernacular. Anyhow, others do it wonderfully well, as testified at Rothbury Festival's poetry readings.

When my companions and I were leaving the Barrels public house late one evening, after a concert, a fellow exclaimed to us that it had been "coostie". He was right; it had been 'bary' – or should that be 'baree'? Or …

Naturally, the need to share what we experience and witness is expressed through the telling. Otherwise, the occasion can fade and be lost to memory. The fox, dead beneath the moon, stays alive in the poem 'Asleep'. Remaining 'alive', in terms of awareness, is all we can aim for in our lives' separate journeys. Without the optimism of expectation we are, figuratively speaking, dead. In 'North Road, Berwick', seeing the elderly gentleman, despite his ailment, perform his tiny dance on the petrol station forecourt, epitomised, for me, the heart's undying urge.

The poems in *Dancing Over Cheviot* are no less than a keeping alive of events and experiences which, inhaled with imagination, were silently translated on to the page.

At Keep Fit sessions in Wooler on Wednesday evenings – ladies' and mens' classes, the enjoyment of our work'out through rhythmic exercise lifts us from the grind of our routine day. Similarly, putting together this second volume of mine has proven both a physical and mental challenge, rewarded by its leap towards line and verse. Now, despite the book itself being finished, as long as the sights, stories and sensations within it continue to be grasped, then I expect the dance, as in the old fellow's brief flight, to be far from over …

Photographs by Kevin Temple complement the following poems:

Cheswick; Lesbury Bridge; Ewartly Shank; Brownridge;
Kettley Stone; Alnwick Music Festival; Cateran's Cave;
Barter Books, Alnwick; Grizzy's Clump; Chattonpark Hill; Past Akeld;
The John Bull, Alnwick; Winter Hunt; Roughting Linn;
Alnwick Market Place; A Happy Man; Snowing; Asleep.
Back cover photo.

Kevin's photographs can be viewed at www.photo.net

Thanks to:

Alistair Anderson, for providing the photograph of Will Atkinson,
Willie Taylor and Joe Hutton.

Carolyn Strangeways, for providing the photograph of her son, Luke.

Elizabeth Dundas, for providing the photograph of her father,
George Wake.

Ian Clarke, for providing the photograph of Wooler cricket team.

Claire Bagness, artist, for her map of the region highlighting
the poems' locations.

Bill Grisdale, for the photograph accompanying Lucky Wooler and
the drawing for Goshawk.

All other photographs: Noel Hodgson.

Index of Poems

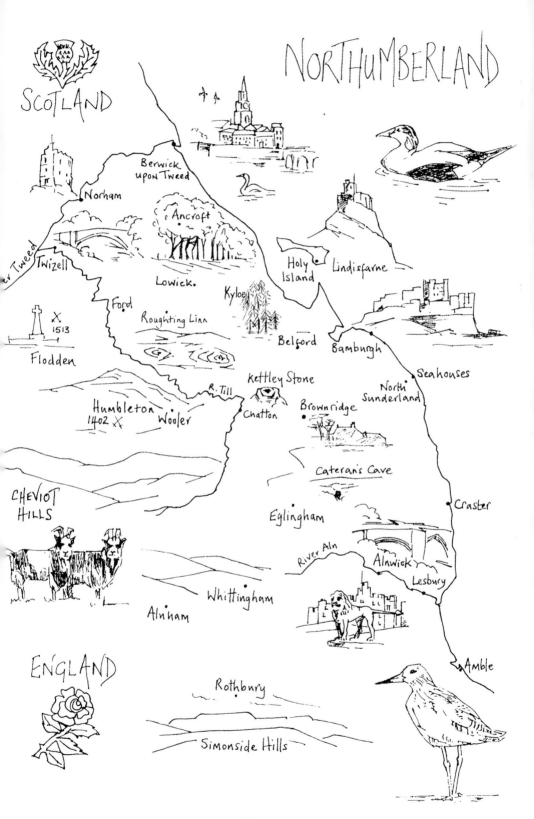

NORTHUMBERLAND

SCOTLAND

Berwick upon Tweed

Norham

Ancroft

Twizell

r Tweed

Ford

Lowick.

Roughting Linn

Kyloe

Holy Island

Lindisfarne

Belford

Bamburgh

Flodden
X 1513

Seahouses

Kettley Stone

North Sunderland

Humbleton 1402 X

Wooler

R. Till

Chatton

Brownridge

Cateran's Cave

CHEVIOT HILLS

Eglingham

Craster

River Aln

Alnwick

Lesbury

Whittingham

Alnham

ENGLAND

Amble

Rothbury

Simonside Hills

122